NINTENDO

BY RACHEL HAMBY

Apex is distributed by North Star Editions:
sales@northstareditions.com | 888-417-0195

Produced for Apex by Red Line Editorial.

Photographs ©: Pixabay/Pexels, cover; Shutterstock Images, 1, 4–5, 6–7, 8, 9, 10–11, 12, 14, 15, 16–17, 18–19, 20, 21, 22–23, 24, 25, 26–27, 29

Library of Congress Control Number: 2022920692

ISBN
978-1-63738-568-5 (hardcover)
978-1-63738-622-4 (paperback)
978-1-63738-725-2 (ebook pdf)
978-1-63738-676-7 (hosted ebook)

Printed in the United States of America
Mankato, MN
082023

NOTE TO PARENTS AND EDUCATORS

Apex books are designed to build literacy skills in striving readers. Exciting, high-interest content attracts and holds readers' attention. The text is carefully leveled to allow students to achieve success quickly. Additional features, such as bolded glossary words for difficult terms, help build comprehension.

TABLE OF CONTENTS

CHAPTER 1

GAME NIGHT 4

CHAPTER 2

NINTENDO BEGINS 10

CHAPTER 3

LOTS OF CONSOLES 16

CHAPTER 4

CREATING GAMES 22

COMPREHENSION QUESTIONS • 28
GLOSSARY • 30
TO LEARN MORE • 31
ABOUT THE AUTHOR • 31
INDEX • 32

GAME NIGHT

A family turns on their Nintendo Switch. They want to play a game called *Mario Kart 8 Deluxe*. One player chooses to race as Mario. Another selects a ghost named King Boo.

Players can choose from 42 different characters in
Mario Kart 8 Deluxe.

Players steer a kart through the track. They try to finish first.

The players speed around a racetrack. Mario hits a mystery block. The block gives him a **power-up**. It's a banana peel!

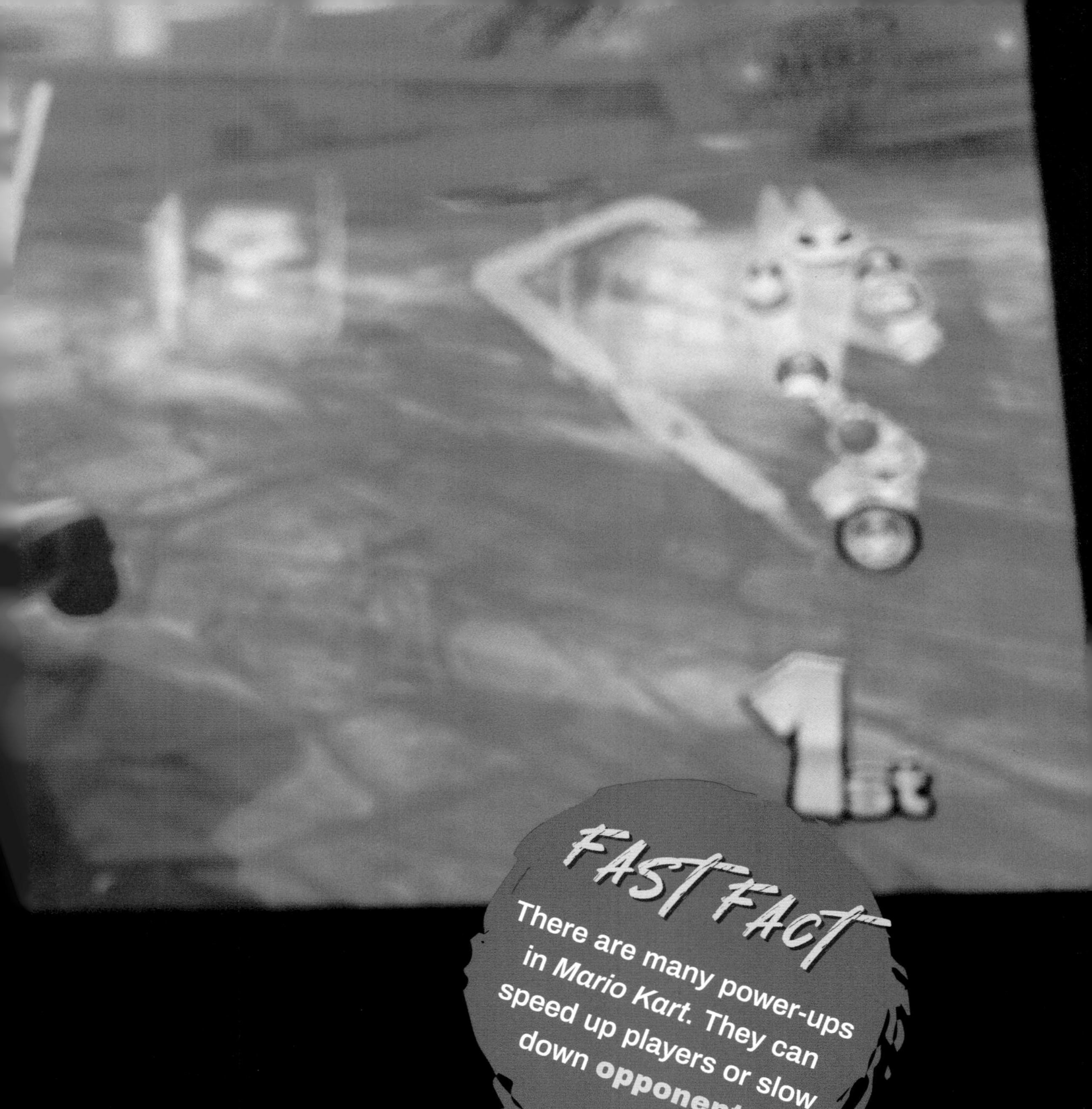

FAST FACT

There are many power-ups in *Mario Kart*. They can speed up players or slow down **opponents**.

Mario Kart players can unlock different karts and parts by completing races.

Mario drops the banana peel. Another player hits it. Their car spins. Mario passes the player and finishes the race in first place.

CRAZY COURSES

In *Mario Kart 8 Deluxe*, players can race on 48 different tracks. Some races go through castles. Other courses are in deserts or mountains.

Mario Kart 8 Deluxe came out in 2017. It became one of the best-selling Switch games.

CHAPTER 2

NINTENDO BEGINS

Fusajiro Yamauchi started Nintendo in 1889. At first, the company made playing cards. In the 1960s, it began making other games.

Nintendo is based in Kyoto, Japan.

In the 1970s, Nintendo started to make **arcade games**. These games had simple **graphics** and controls.

NINTENDO ICONS

The *Donkey Kong* arcade game came out in 1981. It quickly became popular. In 1983, Nintendo released *Mario Bros.* That was the first game named after Mario.

In *Donkey Kong*, a gorilla drops barrels. Players must jump over the barrels to stay alive.

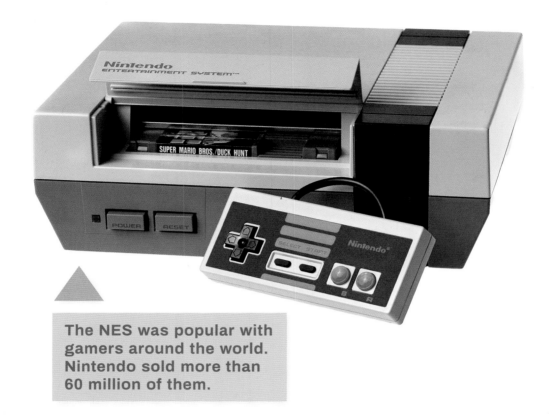

The NES was popular with gamers around the world. Nintendo sold more than 60 million of them.

By 1984, Nintendo fans could play at home. The Nintendo Entertainment System (NES) plugged into a TV. Players could buy **cartridges** for different games.

FAST FACT

Super Mario Bros. was the most popular NES game. Players tried to rescue a princess from a bad guy named Bowser.

People could play more than 700 games on the NES. Several games featured Mario.

CHAPTER 3

LOTS OF CONSOLES

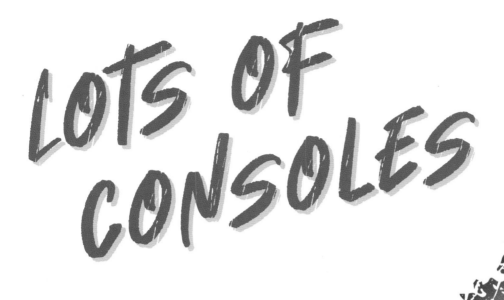

Over time, Nintendo released new and improved **consoles**. The Nintendo 64 had 3D graphics. And the GameCube began using **discs** for games.

The Nintendo 64 was first sold in 1996.

GAME BOY COLOR

Nintendo

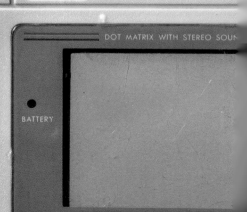

DOT MATRIX WITH STEREO SOUND

BATTERY

Nintendo GAME BOY™

SELECT   START

Nintendo also made handheld systems. In 1989, the company released the Game Boy. It was a huge hit. So, Nintendo made several upgraded versions.

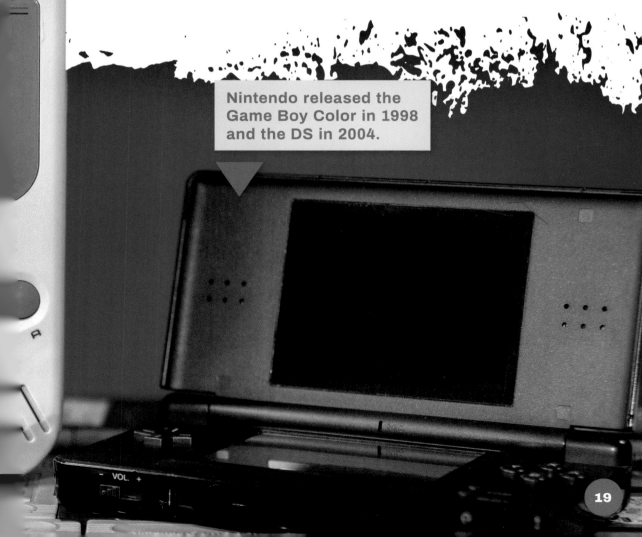

Nintendo released the Game Boy Color in 1998 and the DS in 2004.

The Nintendo Wii senses how players move the controllers.

In 2006, Nintendo introduced the Wii. The console's controllers tracked movement. Players could use them to dance or play sports.

NINTENDO SWITCH

The Nintendo Switch came out in 2017. It let people play a few different ways. Players could use the controllers with a TV. Or they could attach the controllers to the sides of a small screen.

The Nintendo Switch's controllers are called Joy-Cons.

CHAPTER 4

CREATING GAMES

Nintendo makes many popular games. They cover many **genres**. *Animal Crossing* is cute and funny. In *Super Smash Bros.* games, players fight each other.

Animal Crossing: New Horizons came out in 2020. Players build and explore on a deserted island.

Some games are specially designed for certain consoles. *Wii Sports* is one example. Players swing the Wii controllers to play tennis, golf, and other sports.

TOUCHSCREENS

The DS had a touchscreen. Players could tap it with a **stylus**. In *Brain Age*, they could draw and solve problems. In *Nintendogs*, players could pet a dog or throw a ball.

In *Nintendogs*, players use a touchscreen to train and care for pets.

Many Nintendo games are part of a series. For example, *Legend of Zelda* games all feature a character named Link.

The first *Legend of Zelda* game was made for the NES. Later games used newer consoles, such as the Switch.

FAST FACT

Nintendo releases about 20 new games each year.

COMPREHENSION QUESTIONS

Write your answers on a separate piece of paper.

1. Write a few sentences describing the main ideas of Chapter 4.

2. Which Nintendo game would you most like to play? Why?

3. When did Nintendo begin making arcade games?
   - A. the 1960s
   - B. the 1970s
   - C. the 2010s

4. Which Nintendo game tracks players' movements?
   - A. *Donkey Kong*
   - B. *Mario Bros.*
   - C. *Wii Sports*

5. What does **selects** mean in this book?

One player chooses to race as Mario. Another selects a ghost named King Boo.

    A. picks

    B. removes

    C. hides from

6. What does **improved** mean in this book?

Over time, Nintendo released new and improved consoles. The Nintendo 64 had 3D graphics.

    A. older

    B. better

    C. simpler

Answer key on page 32.

GLOSSARY

arcade games
Types of video games people play using large machines.

cartridges
Small plastic boxes that people place in a console to play video games.

consoles
Devices that people use to play video games at home.

discs
Small flat objects that can be used to play video games.

genres
Types or categories of something.

graphics
The images players see during a game.

opponents
Players or characters someone is fighting against.

power-up
A way of gaining extra skills, often for a short time.

stylus
A pen-like tool people use on a touchscreen.

TO LEARN MORE

BOOKS

Abdo, Kenny. *Mario and Luigi: Super Mario Bros Heroes*. Minneapolis: Abdo Publishing, 2021.

Polinsky, Paige V. *Nintendo*. Minneapolis: Bellwether Media, 2023.

Thomas, Rachael L. *Nintendo Innovator: Hiroshi Yamauchi*. Minneapolis: Abdo Publishing, 2019.

ONLINE RESOURCES

Visit **www.apexeditions.com** to find links and resources related to this title.

ABOUT THE AUTHOR

Rachel Hamby lives in the state of Washington. As a tween, she played *Super Mario Bros*. on her cousin's NES. But she never saved Princess Peach.

INDEX

A

Animal Crossing, 22

B

Bowser, 15
Brain Age, 25

D

Donkey Kong, 13

G

Game Boy, 19
GameCube, 16

K

King Boo, 4

L

Legend of Zelda, 26
Link, 26

M

Mario, 4, 6, 8, 13, 15
Mario Kart 8 Deluxe, 4, 7, 9

N

Nintendo 64, 16
Nintendo DS, 18, 25
Nintendo Entertainment
  System (NES), 14, 15
Nintendo Switch, 4, 21

S

Super Smash Bros., 22

W

Wii, 20, 24
Wii Sports, 24

Y

Yamauchi, Fusajiro, 10

ANSWER KEY:
1. Answers will vary; 2. Answers will vary; 3. B; 4. C; 5. A; 6. B